Wolfgang Amadeus Mozart

The Violin Concerti and the Sinfonia Concertante, K. 364

in Full Score

Dover Publications, Inc., New York

Contents

Concerto No. 1 for Violin in B-flat Major, K.207 (composed 1775)   1

    Allegro moderato, 1.   Adagio, 11.   Presto, 16.

Concerto No. 2 for Violin in D Major, K.211 (composed 1775)   27

    Allegro moderato, 27.   Andante, 37.   Rondeau (Allegro), 42.

Concerto No. 3 for Violin in G Major, K.216 (composed 1775)   49

    Allegro, 49.   Adagio, 63.   Rondeau (Allegro), 69.

Concerto No. 4 for Violin in D Major, K.218 (composed 1775)   83

    Allegro, 83.   Andante cantabile, 97.   Rondeau (Andante grazioso — Allegro ma non troppo), 101.

Concerto No. 5 for Violin in A Major, K.219 (composed 1775)   113

    [Allegro aperto], 113.   Adagio, 125.   Tempo di Menuetto, 132.

Sinfonia Concertante for Violin and Viola in E-flat Major, K.364 (composed 1779)   145

    Allegro maestoso, 145.   Andante, 175.   Presto, 187.

Published in Canada by General Publishing Company, Ltd., 30 Lesmill Road, Don Mills, Toronto, Ontario. Published in the United Kingdom by Constable and Company, Ltd.

This Dover edition, first published in 1986, is an unabridged republication of selected sections (Concerti 1–5 for Violin, and the Sinfonia Concertante for Violin and Viola in E-flat Major, K.364) from *Serie 12. Erste Abtheilung. Concerte für Violine und Orchester* from the Complete Works Edition (*Wolfgang Amadeus Mozart's Werke. Kritisch durchgesehene Gesammtausgabe*), originally published by Breitkopf & Härtel, Leipzig, 1877–1883 (items included here: 1877, 1878, 1881).

Manufactured in the United States of America
Dover Publications, Inc., 31 East 2nd Street, Mineola, N.Y. 11501

Library of Congress Cataloging-in-Publication Data

Mozart, Wolfgang Amadeus, 1756–1791.
  [Orchestra music. Selections]
  The violin concerti ; and the Sinfonia concertante, K. 364.

  Reprint. Originally published: Leipzig : Breitkopf & Härtel, 1877–1881 (Wolfgang Amadeus Mozart's Werke. Kritisch durchgesehene Gesammtausgabe. Serie 12)
  Contents: Concerto no. 1 for violin in B-flat major, K. 207 (composed 1775)—Concerto no. 2 for violin in D major, K. 211 (composed 1775)—Concerto no. 3 for violin in G major, K. 216 (composed 1775)—[etc.]
  1. Concertos (Violin)—Scores. 2. Violin and viola with orchestra—Scores. I. Mozart, Wolfgang Amadeus, 1756–1791. Concertos, violin, orchestra. 1986. II. Mozart, Wolfgang Amadeus, 1756–1791. Sinfonie concertanti, violin, viola, orchestra, K. 364, E♭ major. 1986.
M1012.M933D7 1986   86-751165
ISBN 0-486-25169-1

Concerto No. 1 for Violin
in B-flat Major, K.207

2   Concerto No. 1 in B-flat Major

Presto.

Presto.

18   Concerto No. 1 in B-flat Major

20   Concerto No. 1 in B-flat Major

Concerto No. 2 for Violin
in D Major, K.211

28   Concerto No. 2 in D Major

30   Concerto No. 2 in D Major

40   Concerto No. 2 in D Major

Rondeau.

44   Concerto No. 2 in D Major

Concerto No. 3 for Violin
in G Major, K.216

Rondeau.

Andante.

Allegretto.

Tempo I.

Concerto No. 4 for Violin
in D Major, K.218

90 Concerto No. 4 in D Major

94   Concerto No. 4 in D Major

Andante cantabile.

Andante cantabile.

RONDEAU.
Andante grazioso.

Andante grazioso.

Allegro ma non troppo.

Allegro ma non troppo.

104   Concerto No. 4 in D Major

Andante grazioso.

Andante grazioso.

Allegro ma non troppo.

Andante grazioso.

Andante grazioso.

Allegro ma non troppo.

Allegro ma non troppo.

Concerto No. 5 for Violin
in A Major, K.219

SOLO

Tempo di Menuetto.

Oboi.

Corni in A.

Violino principale.

Violino I.

Violino II.

Viola.

Violoncello e Contrabasso.

136   Concerto No. 5 in A Major

144   Concerto No. 5 in A Major

Sinfonia Concertante for Violin and Viola
in E-flat Major, K.364

158   Sinfonia Concertante in E-flat Major